KNOCK-KNOCK JOKES FOR KIDS AND ADULTS FROM 9 TO 90

KNOCK-KNOCK JOKES FOR KIDS AND ADULTS FROM 9 TO 90

101 CLEAN AND WITTY KNOCK-KNOCK JOKES FOR YOUR AMUSEMENT

MARTYN DEMAS

CruGuru

Foreword

I have always enjoyed knock-knock jokes and over time kept a notebook where I wrote down some of my own ideas for these kinds of jokes. This is a compilation of 101 of the best that I could come up with so far. I hope that these jokes would give you just as much enjoyment as I had in thinking them out.

Please note that this book will not be suitable for younger readers, as most of the words will not be in their vocabulary yet

Martyn Demas
December 2013

Table of Contents

1. Get a Doorbell!

1.

Knock-knock...
Who's there?
Aloha
Aloha who?
If you had Aloha bell, I would be able to reach it and ring it.

2.

Knock-knock...
Who's there?
Isabel
Isabel who?
Sorry I knocked, I now see there Isabel next to your door.

3.

Knock-knock...
Who's there?
Candice
Candice who?
Candice bell ring?

4.

Knock-knock...
Who's there?
Unattended
Unattended who?
Unattended to my doorbell. I think she should take a look at yours too.

5.

Knock-knock...
Who's there?
Alison
Alison who?
Alison-ed if your bell worked, but it didn't - that's why I knocked.

6.

Knock-knock...
Who's there?
Anywhere
Anywhere who?
Anywhere is the bell on this door?

7.

Knock-knock...
Who's there?
Mabel
Mabel who?
Mabel is always in working order. You should get yours fixed!

8.

Knock-knock...
Who's there?
Monocles
Monocles who?
Monocles are sore from knocking on your door. Please get a bell!

2. Animal Talk

9.

Knock-knock...
Who's there?
Damien
Damien who?
Damien dog just bit me!

10.

Knock-knock...
Who's there?
Detail
Detail who?
Detail of your dog is stuck in the door!

11.

Knock-knock...
Who's there?
Debbie
Debbie who?
Ouch! Debbie just stung me!

12.

Knock-knock...
Who's there?
Honey bee
Honey bee who?
Honey bee a dear and get me a drink.

13.

Knock-knock...
Who's there?
Demise
Demise who?
Demise have eaten a hole through your door!

14.

Knock-knock...
Who's there?
Oink-oink
Oink-oink who?
What do you want to be? A pig or an owl?

15.

Knock-knock...
Who's there?
Maddox
Maddox who?
Open quick! A bunch of Maddox are chasing me!

16.

Knock-knock...
Who's there?
Amos
Amos who?
Amos-quito just bit me!

17.

Knock-knock...
Who's there?
Debarking
Debarking who?
Debarking of your dog is annoying me!

3. Food-Related

18.

Knock-knock...
Who's there?
Cashew
Cashew who?
Gesundheit!

19.

Knock-knock...
Who's there?
Moderate
Moderate who?
Me and Moderate scrambled eggs for breakfast. Would you also like some?

20.

Knock-knock...
Who's there?
Misapply
Misapply who?
Misapply of sugar is finished - can I borrow some of yours?

21.

Knock-knock...
Who's there?
Displace
Displace who?
Displace gives me the creeps, but I have to deliver your pizza here.

22.

Knock-knock...
Who's there?
Mistake
Mistake who?
Mistake is still raw because my power went out. Can I please use your stove?

23.

Knock-knock...
Who's there?
Announce
Announce who?
Announce of prevention is worth a pound of cure, according to the idiom.

24.

Knock-knock...
Who's there?
Appear
Appear who?
I'm eating appear. Do you also want one?

25.

Knock-knock...
Who's there?
Waiter
Waiter who?
Waiter minute while I just finish my call.

26.

Knock-knock...
Who's there?
Olive
Olive who?
Olive next door. I'm your new neighbor.

27.

Knock-knock...
Who's there?
Justin
Justin who?
Justin time for breakfast!

28.

Knock-knock...
Who's there?
Pete
Pete who?
Pete-za delivery man!

4. People Points

29.

Knock-knock...
Who's there?
Ammonia
Ammonia who?
Ammonia a poor guy standing out here in the cold and rain.

30.

Knock-knock...
Who's there?
Your girlfriend
Your girlfriend who?
How many girlfriends do you have?

31.

Knock-knock...
Who's there?
Little old lady
Little old lady who?
Didn't know you could yodel...

32.

Knock-knock...
Who's there?
Centimeter
Centimeter who?
My sister came to your house and I was centimeter here.

33.

Knock-knock...
Who's there?
Sofa
Sofa who?
Sofa, it's only you and me here.

34.

Knock-knock...
Who's there?
Ivory
Ivory who?
Ivory about you - That's why I decided to come and visit you.

35.

Knock-knock...
Who's there?
Wedlock
Wedlock who?
Wedlock the door when we go out.

36.

Knock-knock...
Who's there?
Aftermath
Aftermath who?
Could we get together aftermath class?

37.

Knock-knock...
Who's there?
Detest
Detest who?
Detest is only on the day after tomorrow. Let's go out now!

5. Real Names

38.

Knock-knock...
Who's there?
Adair
Adair who?
Adair you to open the door.

39.

Knock-knock...
Who's there?
Cassandra
Cassandra who?
Cassandra come outside and play with us?

40.

Knock-knock...
Who's there?
Owen
Owen who?
Owen will you open the door?

41.

Knock-knock...
Who's there?
Obama
Obama who?
I'm Obama self. Can I join you?

42.

Knock-knock...
Who's there?
Agatha
Agatha who?
Agatha old newspapers. Do you perhaps have some for me?

43.

Knock-knock...
Who's there?
Avery
Avery who?
Avery sorry, it's the wrong address.

44.

Knock-knock...
Who's there?
Aiden
Aiden who?
Sorry, Aiden know it was so late.

45.

Knock-knock...
Who's there?
Shelley
Shelley who?
I'm in a real hurry! Shelley start the car so long?

46.

Knock-knock...
Who's there?
Tyler
Tyler who?
Tyler and painter at your service...

47.

Knock-knock...
Who's there?
Dina
Dina who?
Dina tell you to keep your dog in your own yard?

48.

Knock-knock...
Who's there?
Hartley
Hartley who?
You Hartley wasted any time to answer the door - were you ex-pecting someone?

49.

Knock-knock...
Who's there?
Dudley
Dudley who?
Dudley perhaps come by here today?

50.

Knock-knock...
Who's there?
Patton
Patton who?
Give me a Patton the back - I've just won the game!

51.

Knock-knock...
Who's there?
Doris
Doris who?
The Doris stuck on my foot, that's why I knocked!

52.

Knock-knock...
Who's there?
Obed
Obed who?
Obed you don't know who this is!

53.

Knock-knock...
Who's there?
Max
Max who?
Max no difference - just open the door!

54.

Knock-knock...
Who's there?
Willy
Willy who?
Willy mind your own business and let me in!

55.

Knock-knock...
Who's there?
Alberta
Alberta who?
Alberta still in pajamas - that's why you don't want to open the door!

56.

Knock-knock...
Who's there?
Wiles
Wiles who?
Wiles keen to join us.

57.

Knock-knock...
Who's there?
Ivan
Ivan who?
Ivan to come inside!

58.

Knock-knock...
Who's there?
Juno
Juno who?
Do Juno the time, please?

59.

Knock-knock...
Who's there?
Toby
Toby who?
Toby or not to be...

60.

Knock-knock...
Who's there?
Luke
Luke who?
Luke through the keyhole and you will see who.

61.

Knock-knock...
Who's there?
Wendy
Wendy who?
Wendy think you can open the door for me?

62.

Knock-knock...
Who's there?
Arthur
Arthur who?
Athur-got who.

63.

Knock-knock...
Who's there?
Trish
Trish who?
Gesundheid!

64.

Knock-knock...
Who's there?
Matlock
Matlock who?
Matlock the door when you leave.

6. Open This Door!

65.

Knock-knock...
Who's there?
Allowed
Allowed who?
Open this door right now, or I'll make allowed noise outside!

66.

Knock-knock...
Who's there?
Appoint
Appoint who?
You must make appoint of it to answer your door much sooner!

67.

Knock-knock...
Who's there?
Disclosed
Disclosed who?
Disclosed door in front of me is really starting to annoy me now!

68.

Knock-knock...
Who's there?
Anyplace
Anyplace who?
Anyplace your hand on the door handle and just open it!

69.

Knock-knock...
Who's there?
Kernel
Kernel who?
Kernel Evans and Major Lee - open up immediately for your inspection or you'll all go to the detention barracks!

70.

Knock-knock...
Who's there?
Solo
Solo who?
I did not think you would stoop solo as to not wanting to open the door for me!

71.

Knock-knock...
Who's there?
Manure
Manure who?
Manure certainly taking your time to answer the door!

72.

Knock-knock...
Who's there?
Disengagement
Disengagement who?
Disengagement will be over if you don't open the door right now!

73.

Knock-knock...
Who's there?
Canoe
Canoe who?
Canoe please open the door? I'm tired of waiting outside in the cold.

74.

Knock-knock...
Who's there?
Impressed
Impressed who?
Open quickly - Impressed for time!

75.

Knock-knock...
Who's there?
Anyhow
Anyhow who?
Anyhow long are you going to take before you open this door?

76.

Knock-knock...
Who's there?
Unabashed
Unabashed who?
Unabashed my door in when I didn't want to open for her.

77.

Knock-knock...
Who's there?
Well-off
Well-off who?
Well-off I am - it looks like you don't want to open the door for me.

78.

Knock-knock...
Who's there?
Police
Police who?
Police let me in - it is cold outside!

79.

Knock-knock...
Who's there?
Impale
Impale who?
Impale from walking so far. May I come inside?

80.

Knock-knock...
Who's there?
Dawn
Dawn who?
Dawn leave me standing out here in the cold.

81.

Knock-knock...
Who's there?
Imposing
Imposing who?
If imposing as a pizza delivery man, will you open the door for me?

82.

Knock-knock...
Who's there?
Disarm
Disarm who?
Disarm of mine is getting tired of all the knocking!

7. Funny Names

83.

Knock-knock...
Who's there?
Format
Format who?
Is Matt here? I have a package format.

84.

Knock-knock...
Who's there?
Mason
Mason who?
Mason wants to come and play with your son.

85.

Knock-knock...
Who's there?
Dimensioned
Dimensioned who?
Dimensioned that you might be here.

86.

Knock-knock...
Who's there?
Easel
Easel who?
Easel also coming with?

87.

Knock-knock...
Who's there?
Valor
Valor who?
Either Valor Cindy will join us tonight.

88.

Knock-knock...
Who's there?
Compete
Compete who?
Compete, we are going to be late!

89.

Knock-knock...
Who's there?
Manicured
Manicured who?
Manicured my flu today.

8. Last but not Least

90.

Knock-knock...
Who's there?
Diffuse
Diffuse who?
Diffuse in my car has blown. Can I please use your phone?

91.

Knock-knock...
Who's there?
Apart
Apart who?
Apart of me wants to tell you and a part doesn't. Which shall it be?

92.

Knock-knock...
Who's there?
Isolate
Isolate who?
I'm sorry isolate - my car broke down.

93.

Knock-knock...
Who's there?
Design
Design who?
Design in the road is damaged. I need some directions, please.

94.

Knock-knock...
Who's there?
Eiffel
Eiffel who?
Eiffel down and hurt my knee.

95.

Knock-knock...
Who's there?
Spell
Spell who?
W-h-o.

96.

Knock-knock...
Who's there?
Jewel
Jewel who?
I'm well; are jewel too?

97.

Knock-knock...
Who's there?
Deceit
Deceit who?
Deceit of your rocking chair on the porch is wet.

98.

Knock-knock...
Who's there?
Iran
Iran who?
Iran all the way here to visit you.

99.

Knock-knock...
Who's there?
Delight
Delight who?
Delight is still switched on and the sun is shining already!

100.

Knock-knock...
Who's there?
Attack
Attack who?
Ouch, my foot hurts! I just stepped into attack!

101.

Knock-knock...
Who's there?
Itchy
Itchy who?
Gesundheid!

Printed in Poland
by Amazon Fulfillment
Poland Sp. z o.o., Wrocław

51604804R00029